BORN TO BE A COWGIRL

BORN TO BE

A COWGIRL

A SPIRITED RIDE THROUGH THE OLD WEST

CANDACE SAVAGE

TRICYCLE PRESS

BERKELEY, CALIFORNIA

Tricycle Press
P.O. Box 7123
Berkeley, California 94707
www.tenspeed.com

Originated by Greystone Books. Published in the United States of
America by Tricycle Press, Berkeley.

The author gratefully acknowledges the assistance of horsewoman
Norlane Jensen and rancher-writer-historian Thelma Poirier.

LIBRARY OF CONGRESS CATALOGING-IN-PUBLICATION DATA

Savage, Candace Sherk, 1949–
  Born to be a cowgirl : a spirited ride through the old West /
by Candace Savage.
  p. cm.
  Includes bibliographical references and index.
  ISBN 1-58246-019-1 (hardcover) — ISBN 1-58246-020-5 (pbk.)
  1. Cowgirls—West (U.S.)—History—Juvenile literature. 2. Cowgirls—
West (U.S.)—Biography—Juvenile literature. 3. Cowgirls—West
(U.S.)—Anecdotes—Juvenile literature. 4. Ranch life—West (U.S.)—
Juvenile literature. 5. Frontier and pioneer life—West (U.S.)—Juvenile
literature. 6. West (U.S.)—Social life and customs—Juvenile literature.
[1. Cowgirls. 2. Frontier and pioneer life—West (U.S.) 3. West
(U.S.)—Social life and customs] I. Title.

  F596 .S233 2001
  978—dc21

                                                   00-061559

Sources for quoted material appear on page 62.

Every attempt has been made to trace accurate ownership of
copyrighted visual material in this book. Errors and omissions will
be corrected in subsequent editions, provided notification is sent to
the publisher.

Design: Val Speidel
Cover design: Toni Tajima
Front cover: Original image, Buffalo Bill Historical Center,
  Cody, Wyoming
Title page: Denver Public Library, Western Heritage Center
Copyright and contents page: Provincial Archives of Alberta
Printed and bound in Hong Kong by C&C Offset

CONTENTS

BORN IN THE SADDLE

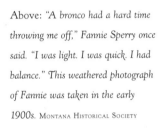

Fannie Sperry admired a horse with spirit. That was why she had decided to buy the bronc that was pacing around the corral at the Herrin ranch. She liked the way his hooves stirred the blue Montana dust; most of all, she admired his strength and his wildness.

The year was 1906, and Fannie was nineteen, a slender young woman with calm, knowing eyes that looked out from under the brim of her Stetson hat. Her entire attention was focused on the outlaw in the corral. He was a mouse-colored roan by the name of Blue Dog, and none of the cowboys on Herrin Ranch could ride him. Get on board that one, they warned her, and you'll end up in the dust. But Fannie wanted to have him, and she was prepared to pay a good price. She had ridden over to the ranch on a gentle, well-trained mare, and she offered her own horse in trade for the unridable Blue Dog.

The cowboys accepted this offer and helped Fannie unsaddle her mare. There was only one small problem. Fannie still had to get back to her family's ranch up in the hills. Since she no longer had a saddle horse, how did she propose to get home?

Not a problem, Fannie decided. She would ride the bronc.

Before anyone could stop her, Fannie picked up her saddle and climbed into the corral. Clucking and murmuring to the horse to calm him, she gently set the saddle on his back, drew the cinch under his belly, and pulled it tight. The men held their breath as Fannie swung onto the horse, but the explosion they were waiting for never happened. Blue

Above: "A bronco had a hard time throwing me off," Fannie Sperry once said. "I was light. I was quick. I had balance." This weathered photograph of Fannie was taken in the early 1900s. MONTANA HISTORICAL SOCIETY

Top left: Ladies' spurs were designed to fit the narrow heel of a woman's boot. Other spurs are shown on pages 23 and 39.

Facing page: Riding at a full gallop, a cowgirl ropes a snorting steer. This illustration was made to advertise a Western movie, around 1900. BUFFALO BILL HISTORICAL CENTER, CODY, WYOMING

Dog heaved and strained against the saddle, but Fannie quickly eased him into a walk. Then she turned that wild horse out of the gate and over the hills toward home.

Horses in Heaven

Fannie Sperry loved horses so much that she couldn't talk about herself without talking about them, too.

I was born March 27, 1887 on a horse ranch at the foot of Bear Tooth Mountain in Montana, and horses have shaped my whole way of life.

Perhaps it is odd that a woman should be born with a deep love of horseflesh, but I have never thought so. To me, it seems as normal as breathing air or drinking water. The biggest thing on my horizon has always been a four-legged critter with mane and tail.

If there are not horses in heaven, I do not want to go there. But I believe there will be horses in heaven, for God loved them or He would not have created them with such majesty.

Facing page: *"I hardly saw men,"* *Fannie Sperry once joked, "yet let a* *horse go down the road and I noted* *all there was to see about it!" This* *young cowgirl appears to share* *Fannie's deep love of horseflesh.* GLENBOW ARCHIVES, CALGARY, ALBERTA NA 335 23

THE CALL OF THE WEST

Fannie Sperry was a cowgirl—one of a remarkable group of ranch women who rode across the prairies of western Canada and the United States, beginning in the mid-nineteenth century. At that time, most people in North America lived in bustling industrial cities like Toronto, Chicago, Montreal, and New York. But as the East became grimy and crowded, people began to look west. Out West, there were no smokestacks, no noise, and no fences. Instead, there was a great, shining sea of grass that supported vast herds of buffalo. These herds, in turn, supported the First Nations people, who relied on the buffalo for every necessity of life—meat for food, bone for tools, hides for clothing and shelter.

To the people in the eastern cities, the West looked like a wilder-

Mr. and Mrs. Charles McKay came from Boston to start a new life as ranchers on the wild Montana prairie. This photo of their spread was taken in 1905 by their neighbor, Evelyn Cameron, who had recently arrived from England. MONTANA HISTORICAL SOCIETY, EVELYN CAMERON PHOTO

ness that could be put to better use. They thought that the First Nations people should be required to settle on small parcels of land called reservations or reserves. After that, the easterners said, the buffalo should be replaced with herds of cattle. Cows would eat the grass of the prairies, and their meat could then be sold back East to the city folks as beefsteaks and roasts. This idea was the beginning of the western cattle business.

For First Nations people, these changes caused painful difficulties. But for the newcomers who moved out onto the plains with their herds of bawling cows, this era marked the beginning of a great adventure. People came by the hundreds to set up ranches on the wide open plains, in territories like Alberta, Montana, Saskatchewan, Wyoming, and Texas. Among the people who answered the call of the West were Fannie Sperry's parents.

Kitsipimi Otunna, a Sarcee woman from southern Alberta, was photographed in the 1890s beside her buffalo-skin tepee. The cowgirls were inspired by the skill and style of First Nations women and did their best to ride "like Indians." PROVINCIAL ARCHIVES OF ALBERTA, ERNEST BROWN PHOTO B51

RUNNING WILD

The Sperrys set up their ranch at the foot of Bear Tooth Mountain in Montana in the 1870s. By then, the First Nations people had been pushed aside and the buffalo were almost gone, but in other ways the prairie lands were much the same as they had been for thousands of years. The wind still swept over hills that were silvered with sage, and meadowlarks made their nests in the prairie wool. Although life in the West was changing, the country had still not been plowed. (That would happen a little later, around 1900, when the ranchers themselves were pushed aside by farmers who came west to plow the land and plant crops.)

The Sperrys were cattle ranchers—they raised cattle to be sold for beef—but they also made money by catching and taming wild horses. These animals were the descendants of Arabian horses that had been shipped to North America from Europe when the Spanish invaded, around 1500. Over the years, many of these horses had escaped from their owners to run wild, and thousands still ranged through the hills around the Sperry ranch. Ranchers like Fannie and her father would round up a few at a time by chasing a small herd of them into a corral. The first few times they were mounted, the horses tried to throw off

Little Kathy Daniothy has been hoisted onto the broad back of the family pig. When a horse was not available, children on pioneer ranches often tried riding calves, steers, sheep, and anything else they could catch.

their riders, but once trained, they became first-rate cow ponies. Hardy enough to withstand the freezing winds of December and the searing heat of July—fast, sure-footed, and strong—they were ideal for working with cattle on the grasslands.

Fannie Sperry was an expert at taming horses because she had grown up with them. When she was just a toddler, a wild horse had wandered down out of the hills to drink from a stream near her house, and she had run after it on her chubby legs, trailing a long scarf. She wanted to catch that horse! Soon her mother (an expert horsewoman herself) decided that Fannie was old enough to ride, so she hoisted her onto a gentle horse and told her not to fall off. When Fannie took a tumble, her mother dusted her off, popped her back in the saddle, and told her to do better next time. That was the beginning and end of Fannie's riding instruction.

On the dry hills above the Yellowstone River, Montana ranch woman Janet Williams poses with her favorite horse, Zip, in this 1911 photograph. Montana Historical Society, Evelyn Cameron photo

Some cowgirls began learning to ride before they could even walk. Tiny children were sometimes plopped onto the back of a reliable horse and tied to the saddlehorn as a way of keeping them out of trouble. When the adults were all too busy to keep an eye on the kids, that old horse became the babysitter.

Cowgirl Tad Lucas cradles her baby daughter, Mitzi, in her ten-gallon hat. When not in use as a baby carrier, the cowhand's wide-brimmed hat provided protection from sun, wind, and rain.
NATIONAL COWGIRL HALL OF FAME, FORT WORTH, TEXAS

Buster's Biscuits

For a little girl of five, getting up onto a horse could be a big challenge. But an Arizona cowgirl named Georgie Sicking had the answer.

For my fifth birthday [in 1926], my dad bought an eight-year-old gelding, Morgan and Thoroughbred breeding. He had been raised as a pet and was fond of biscuits. I would take a biscuit to where he was, drop it on the ground, and when he put his head down to get it, I would climb on his head, crawl up his neck, and be on his back. I could turn him by slapping his neck, and stop him by pretending to fall off. I owned him for twenty years, until he died. I named him Buster.

Life on a frontier ranch was lived on horseback. According to Agnes Morley, who grew up on a spread in New Mexico in the 1880s, it was unthinkable to be caught walking anywhere. "In fact," she recalled, "one must never be seen afoot except in the business of looking for a horse."

Once a child was past the baby stage (when she had to stick to old plugs), she was allowed to ride any horse that she could get hold of. Bareback or saddled up, it didn't matter which. Agnes remembered overhearing an argument about whether or not it was safe for her to ride a "long-legged cayuse" named Roadrunner. She'd get bucked off, one cowboy objected. Didn't matter, another hand said. The horse wasn't likely to run away, so she'd be able to catch him and get on again. That, Agnes remembered, was the only criterion. "Other than a reasonable hope—and this point was often strained—that we could stay on the horse at all, there were no standards set for our mounts. Horses of every temperament and every sort of habit, good or bad, were considered 'safe.' We took whatever horseflesh was at hand."

"I can't imagine how it was that we had such freedom," another cowgirl said. "I suppose our parents thought there was nothing in the

Dreaming of the day when she will have a horse of her own, this cowgirl takes her doll for a ride. The sawhorse on which they are mounted was used to prepare the huge pile of firewood in the background. Firewood was burned both for cooking and heating the house. GLENBOW ARCHIVES, CALGARY, ALBERTA NC 39 290

Let's Race!

Thelma Poirier, who still lives on a ranch in southern Saskatchewan, remembers a day when she and her sister Marjorie went riding over the hills with two of their cousins. The four girls rode bareback, double, on horses named Teddy and Nellie.

Mama said not to race, but we race anyway. Teddy goes faster and faster, my pigtails fly out behind me and the plaid ribbons blow in the wind. Teddy is chopping up the grass, pounding holes in the hills. He is making as much noise as a hundred horses. Teddy and Nellie run faster and faster until they are winded.

  We are home again. My overalls twist around and between my legs when I slide off Teddy's back. They are plastered with horse hair and the cloth is stuck to my legs. Marjorie jumps down and slips the bridle off Teddy. He rolls in the loose dirt in front of the barn, first one way and then the other, then he sits on his haunches and shakes some of the dirt away. Finally he pushes up with his hind legs and races off to find the other horses in the pasture.

Valley that could hurt us, and if we were on our horses and gone at least we weren't under foot. Our parents didn't realize, of course, that we were all doing very dangerous things. We raced our horses across the Valley floor, through prairie-dog towns, and across ditches. We swam in the river . . . We climbed the cap rock on the Black Mesa," with its precipitous cliffs. It was a wonder that none of those children was badly hurt or even killed.

For children who grew up on the western range, riding wild horses through a wild landscape was as natural as getting out of bed. "You know, everybody says we've led such an interesting life," one cowgirl remarked. "But it wasn't unusual to us. That's what we had to do, so we did it."

COWGIRL GEAR

The cowgirls applied this same practical thinking to choosing their riding gear. In those days, women were expected to use a side-saddle—a device that permitted riders to wear skirts and sit with their legs modestly together. The saddle consisted of a flat, slippery seat and a post, or saddlehorn, that the lady curled one leg around so both of her legs rested on the same side of the horse. This equipment might

Calamity Jane, by Herself

Calamity Jane was one of the most famous of the early cowgirls. A well-known character in Montana and Wyoming, she was remembered by her neighbors both for her skills as a horsewoman and for her kindness to the sick during a flu epidemic. Sadly, she was also a heavy drinker, who was sometimes reduced to supporting herself by selling pamphlets about her accomplishments. This is an excerpt from her "Life and Adventures."

My maiden name was Martha Cannary, was born in Princeton, Missouri, May 1st, 1852. As a child I always had a fondness for adventure and out-door exercise and especial fondness for horses which I began to ride at an early age and continued to do so until I became an expert rider being able to ride the most vicious and stubborn of horses, in fact the greater portion of my early times was spent in this manner.

In 1865 we moved from Missouri to Virginia City, Montana, taking five months to make the journey. While on the way, I was at all times with the men when there was excitement and adventure to be had. By the time we reached Virginia City I was considered a remarkable good shot and a fearless rider for a girl of my age.

[Mother died, 1866. Father died, 1867. Joined the army as a scout in 1870.] Up to this time I had always worn the costume of my sex. When I joined the army I donned the uniform of a soldier. It was a bit awkward at first but I soon got to be perfectly at home in men's clothes.

I returned to Montana in 1882 and took up a ranch on the Yellow Stone River, raising stock and cattle. Hoping this little history of my life may interest all readers. I remain as in the older days, Mrs. M. Burk, Better Known As Calamity Jane.

have been fine for a trot around a city park, but it was not much use when you were trying to stay on the back of a bucking bronc. The cowgirls quickly decided to switch to western saddles and ride like the men.

If the cowgirls were going to ride astride, they needed suitable clothes. They couldn't be flapping and dragging around in long skirts and petticoats. The standards of the time called for skirts right down to the ground, so that a girl's legs were completely covered. (Even showing an ankle was considered rude.) The cowgirls did not want to start a scandal, but they needed to move their legs, so they came up with a compromise. They began to wear split-skirts, or "California riding costumes"—garments that were a cross between skirts and pants.

Even this modest clothing sent some people into shock. When a rancher named Evelyn Cameron wore her split-skirt into Miles City, Montana, in 1895, she was warned that it was against the law for women to wear "divided garments" in town. "After riding in forty-eight miles from the ranch, I was much amused at the laughing and giggling girls who stood staring at my costume as I walked about," she said.

In time, ranch girls and women threw caution to the wind and started wearing breeches, pants, and overalls. "I turned a deaf ear to my mother's long-winded lectures upon the conduct of, and correct clothing

Above: *This ranch woman looks calm and confident, with her legs astride her horse and her feet planted deep in the stirrups. She carries a gun for shooting wolves and bears, and a rope for catching cattle that have strayed too far.* Library of Congress USZ62 41449 215101

Facing page: *In this famous photograph, Calamity Jane wears a fringed jacket and pants made of hard-wearing buckskin.* Buffalo Bill Historical Center, Cody, Wyoming

for, 'little ladies,'" one cowgirl recalled. "I cared not a whit for social customs, and could not understand a world designed especially for privileged little boys to romp in, to enjoy sports and play, [privileges that were] sternly denied to 'little ladies.' With spirit and determination, I wore my befringed, buckskin breeches.

"The grown-up's agony over such 'disgraceful apparel' was pathetic," she said. "But I brushed off their ridicule." What mattered was having the freedom to gather a bunch of wild horses or rope a long-horned cow. The cowgirl had work to do.

Right: *For working the range, nothing could compare with the ease of a western saddle. This portrait of the exuberant May Lillie dates from 1908.*
BUFFALO BILL HISTORICAL CENTER, CODY, WYOMING

Facing page: *What mattered was freedom! Evelyn Cameron, who was a photographer as well as a rancher, set up this dare-devil photo and then had someone else snap the shutter for her.*
MONTANA HISTORICAL SOCIETY, EVELYN CAMERON PHOTO

I CAN DO THAT!

A hundred years ago, women and girls were expected to work inside their homes. They were supposed to cook meals, bake bread, wash dishes, do laundry, scrub floors, and look after the children. If they wanted fresh air, they could pull weeds in the garden or gather eggs from the chicken coop. In their spare time (if they had any), they were supposed to sit quietly and mend clothes or embroider cushion covers and samplers for the parlor.

Some women liked these rules, but many others did not. They wanted the freedom to do any job that needed to be done. Montana ranch woman Evelyn Cameron, for example, did housework because she had to, but she worked outdoors because she loved it. "Manual labor is about all I care about," she wrote in a letter to a friend. "After all, it is what will really make a strong woman. I like to break colts, brand calves, cut down trees, ride horses and work in a garden."

A girl who wanted to work with cattle and horses had a hard time getting a job. Many people felt it was not quite decent for a girl to get paid for doing a "man's" work. But if she did the very same tasks without drawing a wage, people did not get so upset—especially if she was helping her father or her husband. Most cowgirls worked on the family ranch. They did the same work as the hired hands but without pay.

Some girls and women found another way to bend the rules about women's work. They ran ranches of their own. Many became ranchers through necessity rather than choice, by inheriting the family spread

Facing page: Although Evelyn Cameron preferred to work outdoors with her horses, she also did "women's work" in the kitchen. Here she kneads a batch of bread dough that she will bake in the wood-burning stove behind her. This photo was taken in 1904.
MONTANA HISTORICAL SOCIETY, EVELYN CAMERON PHOTO

Below: Sebina Jacobson and Johanna Solberg each had land of her own near a town called Square Deal, Alberta.
GLENBOW ARCHIVES, CALGARY, ALBERTA
NA 206 27

The Day Dinner Was Late

On May 1, 1897, Evelyn Cameron wrote these notes in her diary, describing the work she had done that day.

Arose at 6:50. [Made a fire in the woodstove.] Milked. [Cooked] breakfast 8:15. Swept. Washed up. Took setting hen off eggs etc. Watered 3 foals. Carted manure from old corral, took 6 loads to the garden before lunch at 2:15. To work again at 3. Worked, carting manure, till 7:45 at night. I watered foals & had difficulty getting two into the stable, it was rather dark. Under the corral manure there ran an inch layer of snow, hauled it all away. [Prepared] supper 8:45. Thin beaten steak, mince, poached eggs, rice, tomatoes, coffee, pears. Washed up. Wrote diary. Ewen [her husband] was rather put out that dinner was so late.

when their husbands died. A few had to manage as best they could after their husbands left them. But other women established their own ranches because it was what they wanted to do. One of them, Lizzie Johnson Williams of Austin, Texas, got her start by teaching school, doing bookkeeping, and writing sensational romance stories for a magazine; she then used her earnings to purchase cattle and land. "She was smart," one cattleman acknowledged. "Knew cattle; knew when to buy and when to sell. She always bought good stock." At her death in 1924, aged eighty-one, Lizzie left behind a small fortune in cash, real estate, and diamonds.

Lizzie Williams saw herself as a businesswoman and manager who

Because their father was away on business for half the year, the three Buckley sisters ran the family's horse ranch in Montana in the early 1900s. The sister at left has thrown her lariat around the neck of a horse, while one of her sisters comes running, rope in hand, to single out another of the galloping herd. MONTANA HISTORICAL SOCIETY, EVELYN CAMERON PHOTO

Clever, strong-willed Lizzie Williams was one of Texas's most successful cattle dealers. She lived from 1843 to 1924. Austin History Center, Austin Public Library PICB01490

made decisions about how the ranch should be run, but she did not do much of the physical work of looking after the cattle. She hired a foreman and a staff of cowboys to do the dirty work: shooting predators such as coyotes and wolves, building and repairing fences, rounding up strays, assisting the cows with difficult births, selecting the cattle that were ready for sale, feeding and watering the horses, trimming their hooves, doctoring them when they were sick, as well as a thousand other things. But some women ranchers preferred to run the operation by themselves, without the help of a foreman. They not only made the management decisions about when to buy and sell their cattle, but they also did their fair share of the physical labor. "I have tried every kind of work this ranch affords," one woman wrote, "and I can do any of it. I just love to experiment, to work, and to prove out things, so that ranch life and 'roughing it' just suit me."

"I was on my own," another woman rancher recalled. The men on the neighboring ranches thought they knew everything and were always spouting advice. "But they wasn't bossing me. They must have thought I was a tough old sassy thing, but I didn't care what they thought. I had to fight my own battles. I didn't ask them for help."

WILLIE THE KID

Although people sometimes made a fuss about "men's" and "women's" work, the cattle did not care. "The cattle business in those days was conducted on horseback," one ranch woman explained. "Any rider who knew what to do was the equal of any other rider who knew what to do." A skilled young cowgirl could be the best hand on the range.

With her horse saddled and ready to go, Evelyn Cameron pauses to milk one of her cows. In the middle of the corral, her chickens scratch for the grain that she has thrown out for them to feed on. This photo was taken in 1904. MONTANA HISTORICAL SOCIETY, EVELYN CAMERON PHOTO

A cowboy named Sam Houston learned this simple fact firsthand. In 1884, he was moving a herd of cows across the prairies to a distant town, where he hoped to sell them as beef. To get them to market, the cattle had to be made to walk, day after day, for several months. Houston had a crew of cowboys who rode behind the herd on horseback to keep them moving along. This was called driving the cattle. At night, the saddle-weary cowboys camped out on the open prairie, in fair weather and foul. The work was considered unsuitable for girls and women.

One day, Houston decided he needed to add another cowhand to his crew. Nobody was around except a young kid named Willie Matthews, so Houston hired him.

Willie turned out to be a model cowboy. As Houston remembered it, "the kid would get up on the darkest stormy nights and stay with the cattle until the storm was over. He was good natured, very modest, didn't use any swear words or tobacco, and was always pleasant. I was so pleased with him I wished many times that I could find two or three more like him."

Then one evening, Houston and the rest of the crew were sitting around camp. Suddenly, they saw a girl, "all dressed up," walking across the prairie toward them. "Our eyes were all set on her," Houston said, "every man holding his breath. When she got up within about twenty feet of me, she began to laugh, and said, 'You don't know me, do you?'

"Well, for one minute," Houston recalled, "I couldn't speak. She reached her hand out to me, to shake hands, and I said, 'Kid, is it possible that you are a lady?' " And, of course, she was. His favorite cowboy had been a cowgirl all along.

Willie—or was it Wilma?—Matthews had often heard the cowboys talk about the adventure of driving cattle. When they told her that girls were not allowed to go, she had decided to dress up as a boy. She knew she could do the work and was determined to have a chance. "I'm glad I found you," she told Houston as she prepared to ride back home, "for I have enjoyed myself."

HOME ON THE RANGE

A young woman didn't have to join a cattle drive in order to prove what she could do. Everyday life at home on the ranch was full of challenge. Any child who could reach the horse's mane and hold on by herself was ready to become a working rider. One cowgirl remembered that her first job—at the age of three—was to ride out to the pasture, gather the milk cows, and bring them back to the barn for milking. "I had to ride bareback because my Daddy wouldn't let me use a saddle. He was afraid I'd get tangled up and get hurt." A child of five or six might be sent to a neighboring ranch, a few hours' ride away, to carry messages or pick up the mail.

There were two other jobs that seemed especially suited to young cowhands. One was getting out of bed at dawn and traipsing over the prairie on foot to find and catch the horses. "It was routine to bring all the horses from the pasture into the home corral before breakfast," rancher Agnes Morley reports. "In those early years of the open range, when fences were few and everybody's livestock wandered at will, hunting horses consumed a disproportionate amount of time." And once the horses had been gathered in and everyone was fed, the children were often sent out again to look for the cattle. Was the herd finding enough water? Which direction were they headed? Had any of them become bogged down in mud-holes, where they might suffocate

or starve? Should one of the adults ride over and try to pull them out? Since cattle were the family's livelihood, this information had a real dollars-and-cents importance.

A young cowhand was also expected to keep an eye open for mavericks—calves without a brand. Every livestock owner had his or her own registered mark that was scorched into the hide of horses and cows as a proof of ownership. An unmarked calf was easy prey for thieves, so it was important to get the brands in place as early as possible. Most calves were branded at a big roundup in the spring—the most exciting event of the year—when all the cattle in that part of the country were gathered up and driven to the branding corrals. In the days before fences, when livestock roamed freely, cattle belonging to several owners were brought together in one big mooing, milling herd of bulls, steers, barren cows, and cows with calves. (Since the cattle traveled together in mixed herds, it was simpler to round them all up, even the ones that were already branded.)

The first task of the roundup riders was to bring order to this squalling chaos of hooves and dust. Riding calmly through the cattle herd, cowhands on skilled horses maneuvered the animals into smaller groups, sorting them first by brand and then forming separate groups of cows with calves. Cattle kept trying to sprint away and rejoin the main group, but the cowhands were poised to chase them back and keep them where they belonged. Finally, each band of cows and calves was forced into a holding pen, and the calves were then hustled down a passageway into the main corral to be branded.

The instant a calf spurted out of the chute, it was brought to a sudden halt by the loop of a lariat. Another instant and the calf was panting on the ground with its hooves tightly bound together. If the calf was a male, there was the flash of a knife and a squeal as it was castrated. Then came the nostril-curling stench of burned hair as the brand was

Stopped short by a loop of rope, this calf is about to have its feet tied securely together by cowhand Joyce Burton. The calf will be held for a few minutes to be vaccinated, castrated, or branded—then turned loose to rejoin its mother. National Archives of Canada, Richard Wright photo PA116129

Branding with Billie

Monica Hopkins was a city girl who moved to a ranch in Alberta in 1909. This is an excerpt from a letter she wrote to a friend.

I am afraid that I spend more time than I should outside with Billie [her husband], helping him when I can. I have heated branding irons in a fire while Billie roped and tied a calf that he is turning out on the range with its mother. Billie says it doesn't hurt the animal very much if the iron is good and red, but I don't know. I'd hate to have it done to me. But I must confess that it doesn't seem to bother the animal very much after the first jump; just as soon as they are turned out, their first idea is to nibble at the grass.

A Brand of One's Own

Women have owned cattle since the earliest days of western settlement. These eight brands were used to identify cattle owned by Texas women in the 1800s.

 Lise Ardain

 Melanie Martin

 Marie Adelaide Mouton

 Sally Parrott

 Sarah Patello

 Marguerite Richard

 Sarah Smith

 Ana Young

burned into the animal's hide with a kind of metal stamp attached to a long rod. This iron was heated in a fire and pressed against the animal's side until the hair sizzled off, leaving the brand's design. Some cowgirls didn't like branding because they worried about hurting the calves. But others just got on with the job, because they knew that somebody had to do it.

BREAKING WILD HORSES

There was another kind of ranch work that many cowgirls loved—breaking horses. *Breaking* is a violent word, and it is true that some of the old methods of training horses were cruel. A spirited bronco might be whipped or raked with spurs, the sharp spikes that riders wore on the heels of their boots. Some ranchers thought that a stubborn horse should be starved until it gave in. Others pushed their fingers deep into a "bad" horse's eyes as a punishment.

Cruelty to horses made some ranch women very angry. On July 3, 1894, Evelyn Cameron made this entry in her journal: "Saw a cowboy named Drew breaking broncs in the most brutal manner, scaring them into barbed wire & tumbling them on their heads."

Evelyn found such tactics sickening; her own were much gentler. One day, for example, she was leading two young foals across the yard

for water when they suddenly took fright. They were startled by the laundry she had hung on the clothesline to dry. To teach the horses not to shy, she led them back and forth under the billowing clothes. "The little grey foal was awfully willful, threw itself down & skinned my fingers," she wrote in her journal. "So I bandaged them up, put gloves on & led one foal at a time. I had a hard battle with Figs [the iron grey foal] to get her to go under the line, but got both finally so that they let the clothes flap all round them." Another day, after struggling to lead a foal that "fought like a demon," her fingers were "so split" that she could hardly write.

Rather than risk injury to their hands, the Brander sisters, who ran the Dog Creek Canyon Ranch in Montana, preferred to let a horse do the heavy work. Instead of leading an untrained foal around by a rope,

Because many ranchers thought of branding as men's work, women only occasionally worked on branding crews. These cowhands look so clean and neat that it seems possible the photo was staged. COLORADO HISTORICAL SOCIETY

they tied the rebellious youngster to the saddlehorn of an experienced horse. But this method took time, and some horse-breakers couldn't afford to wait. Elsie and Amy Cooksley of Wyoming, for example, didn't "mess around [with] leading horses or anything else. We just got on them and bucked them out. As soon as we got the worst of the buck out of them, which was just two or three days, we took them right out on the range and put them to work. And they made a lot better stock horses that way."

No matter how you looked at it, the work was dangerous. But, as Fannie Sperry once explained, "you just forget about being scared when you ride a [bucking] horse. Think of staying on top and perhaps you shall, some of the time. Just be thankful if you're able to get up and try it once more." That was the greatest thrill a cowgirl could hope for.

Above: *Slopping and sliding around in a muddy corral, Alberta rancher Monica Hopkins takes the first steps in breaking a young horse.* Glenbow Archives, Calgary, Alberta NA397 16

Facing page: *Some cowgirls translated their skill at breaking horses into new careers as bronc riders in the rodeo. In this 1919 photo, professional bronc rider Kitty Canutt enjoys a wild ride aboard a horse named Winarmucca.* Library of Congress LC USZ62 99834

THE WILD BUNCH

For cowgirls, it was hard to draw a line between work and play. Work meant racing across the prairie on a galloping horse or catching a runaway calf in a swirling loop of rope. It meant climbing onto the back of a wild-eyed bucking bronc and taking a chance that you would fly off.

When cowboys and cowgirls were in the mood for fun, they couldn't think of anything more exciting than their everyday work. So they turned their favorite chores into "ranch sports." They held horse races and roping contests to see who was the fastest and best. They dared one another to ride broncs and bulls and to wrestle with long-horned steers. Everyone on the ranch would gather around the corral on a Saturday afternoon to watch the competition and cheer for their favorites.

These playful contests were the beginning of the rodeo. By 1897, when the first major competition was held in Cheyenne, Wyoming, the rodeo was already well on its way to becoming an organized sport, with paying spectators, prizes, and printed programs. But there were few events on the schedule for girls or women. Although everyone knew that the cowgirls loved to rope and ride, the organizers thought that rough-and-tumble events like riding broncs should be only for men.

The cowgirls wanted to share in the excitement. But when they asked for a chance to compete in bronc riding and other events, nobody

Facing page: *Cowgirls fly off their bucking broncs in this rodeo poster from the 1940s. The first rodeo cowgirls liked to call themselves the "Wild Bunch."* LIBRARY OF CONGRESS LC USZC4 1508

Below: *Outfitted in woolly chaps (leg protectors), this cowgirl is ready to rodeo.* BUFFALO BILL HISTORICAL CENTER, CODY, WYOMING

paid attention. So, in 1904, a young Colorado rancher named Bertha Kapernick took matters into her own hands by entering herself in a bronc-riding contest at Cheyenne. (The rule book said that men could compete, but it failed to say that women could not.) Although she did not win the contest, she did win the hearts of the crowd with a dazzling display of skill. "The great multitude cheered," the local newspaper said, for "this extraordinary young lady who has conquered the west."

Bertha Kapernick had made her point, and when the next major rodeo was held in 1906, ladies' bronc riding was on the program. Then, just a few years later, she and the other cowgirls had an even better chance to impress the world with their talents.

The Joy of Living

In the early 1900s, girls were constantly cautioned against taking part in active sports. For one thing, ladies were not supposed to sweat or get dirty. For another, they were expected to protect their reproductive systems from injury and stress. (The experts said that if a girl overexerted herself in sport she would never be able to have children.) By participating in rodeo, young women thumbed their noses at these concerns. One cowgirl, May Lillie, went so far as to recommend bronc riding as the perfect form of exercise for all women.

Let any normally healthy woman who is ordinarily strong screw up her courage and tackle a bucking bronc, and she will find the most fascinating pastime in the field of feminine athletic endeavor. There is nothing to compare, to increase the joy of living, and once accomplished, she'll have more real fun than any pink tea or theater party or ballroom ever yielded.

THE CALGARY STAMPEDE

In the summer of 1912, Fannie Sperry was on her family's Montana ranch when she received a letter:

Dear Miss Sperry,
I'm impressed with your bronc riding. If you can come to the Stampede I'm putting on in Calgary in September, I'm sure you can win some big money. You'll be riding for the world's championship.
Yours truly,
Guy Weadick

Guy Weadick was an entertainer who was well known throughout the West as a cowboy singer and performer. In 1912 he was helping to organize the biggest rodeo the world had ever seen, the first Calgary Stampede. In addition to all the usual competitions, Weadick planned a full program of events for girls and women. His own wife, who competed under the name of Florence (or Flores) La Due, was entered in the ladies' trick-and-fancy-roping contest, a sport that provided a double challenge. For a start, competitors tried to dazzle the judges by catching one or more running horses in a single loop of rope—some ropers could nab ten animals with one throw. For the second part of the event, they were required to spin their ropes into showy loops and twists, both on the ground and from the saddle.

Bertha Kapernick (by now married and known as Bertha Blancett) was planning to compete against Florence in the roping events. In addition, the irrepressible Bertha had also decided to take part in trick riding, bronc riding, and the relay race. Trick riding was a kind of gymnastic display in which riders did headstands and other risky maneuvers on the back of a galloping horse. The object was to look both graceful and daring.

Bronc riding, by contrast, appeared to be a struggle between rider and horse, but it actually called for the skills of a gymnast. Rather than trying to master the horse, the trick was to ride out the storm by fighting to keep your balance and concentration. Since contestants could

Top left: *In a move that demonstrates her agility and strength, fancy roper Florence La Due turns the world upside down and still keeps her rope spinning around. This stunt is called a flat forward spin.* Glenbow Archives, Calgary, Alberta na 628 4

only hold on with one hand, bronc riders had to anchor themselves with their legs. Women were permitted to hobble their stirrups—tie them together under the horse—to provide a solid foundation that supposedly made it easier to stay on. But hobbling was frowned upon by the judges, and riders who performed slick—with their stirrups free—always had a winning advantage.

Bertha Blancett's final event was the relay race, an exciting contest in which riders screamed down the track, came to a sudden stop, then saddled up a second horse, and galloped off. (Sometimes, instead of

With a mighty throw of her lariat, this trick-roping cowgirl has captured six horses in her loop. Buffalo Bill Historical Center, Cody, Wyoming, Burke and Atwell photo

dismounting, relay racers were allowed to leap from one horse to the next, a move they described as "flying.")

Weadick had assembled a knockout program for his stampede, with a full slate of contests, top-notch competitors, and a head-spinning array of prizes. The winner of the ladies' bronc-riding contest, for example, would receive $1,000 (as much as a ranch hand could earn in three or four years). It was an offer that Fannie Sperry and the other cowgirls couldn't refuse, so they packed up their gear and headed for Calgary.

THRILLS AND SPILLS

Although Fannie was entered in the relay race, her best hope of a big win was in the ladies' bronc-riding competition. The contest was to be held over three days, with three rides for each contestant, and the cowgirl with the highest combined score would take home the prizes. To win, she not only had to stay on her mounts and show a little flair; she also had to hope for broncs that had a temper. The rides were scored out of one hundred points each—half for the rider and half

Above: Her feet balanced in special straps, trick rider Tillie Baldwin flies around the arena. Instead of a cumbersome split-skirt, she wears bloomers—short, baggy pants that draw together below the knees.

Facing page: In the 1890s, a western entertainer called Pawnee Bill organized a bronc-riding competition between cowgirls from the U.S. ("western girls") and Mexico ("Mexican señoritas"). The star of his show was Señorita Rosalia.

PAWNEE BILL'S HISTORIC WILD WEST
AMERICA'S NATIONAL ENTERTAINMENT

BEAUTIFUL DARING WESTERN GIRLS AND MEXICAN SEÑORITAS IN A CONTEST OF EQUINE SKILL.

WINNIPEG
STAMPEDE
1913.

for the horse—so there would be no glory if the broncs refused to buck. But the horses were assigned at random, and in the first go-round, Fannie drew a deadbeat nag that jolted across the arena in a series of tame little hops. Alberta cowgirl Goldie St. Clair was more fortunate. She came out on a muscular sorrel named Red Wing, a horse that had accidentally killed a cowboy just days before the Stampede. The crowd gasped as the golden-haired girl whipped and swayed on the back of the plunging bronc, her free arm thrashing through the air and her feet planted deep in hobbled stirrups. After day one, Goldie St. Clair looked like a winner.

Day two brought a reversal. Goldie drew a meek little horse that scarcely bothered to buck, while Fannie sailed out on a wildcat of a bronc named Nett. Day three dawned with Fannie in second place and one more ride to go—one last chance to impress the judges. She waited as the other cowgirls came out on their bucking mounts; she listened as the audience went wild with applause. Then, a voice on the loudspeaker called out her name. "Fannie Sperry," the voice said, "will ride Red Wing." A sudden hush fell over the arena as Fannie straddled the chute and eased herself onto the horse. Then out she came in a blur of

Left: *Hair ribbons flying, Fannie Sperry enjoys a wild ride at the Winnipeg Stampede in 1913.* BUFFALO BILL HISTORICAL CENTER, CODY, WYOMING

Facing page: *With her free hand waving jauntily and stirrups unhobbled, Fannie keeps her seat on a plunging horse named Dismal Disk. This photo was taken in 1920, a few months after Fannie turned thirty-three; she was still riding broncs in her fifties.* MONTANA HISTORICAL SOCIETY

heaving horseflesh and flying hooves. Her free arm kept time with the action; her stirrups swung free.

A few minutes later, the judges announced their choice. Miss Fannie Sperry was the Lady Bucking Horse Champion of the World and the winner of a hand-tooled leather saddle, a gold buckle for her belt—and $1,000.

What's in a Name?

Rodeo cowgirls admired and respected the bucking horses that gave them such rough rides. Fannie Sperry, for instance, had a soft spot for a roan called Silver Tail. "She was a fine bucking horse," Fannie recalled, "and always put on a good show in the arena." Among the other memorable broncs she rode in her rodeo career were Memphis Blues, Morning Glory, Highpockets, Little Swede, Bonehead, Midnight—"probably the toughest bronc I ever rode"—and, of course, Blue Dog, "one of my favorite saddle broncs for years."

Trick-riding and stunt horses also hold a special place in the history of rodeo. Among the most famous were White Man, ridden and trained by Lucille Mulhall, Boy (Florence Hughes Randall), King Tut (Bonnie Gray), and Candy Lamb (Tad Lucas).

Rodeo cowgirl Bonnie Gray earned extra money by jumping over automobiles. On her wedding day in 1925, she and King Tut leaped over a car in which her new husband and her maid of honor were seated.

THE BEGINNING OF THE END

The Calgary Stampede of 1912 marked the beginning of a great new era for rodeo cowgirls. The rodeo was growing—new shows were springing up all across the West—and most of them now included events for girls and women. People came by the hundreds to see champs like Fannie Sperry, Florence La Due, and Bertha Blancett. The cowgirls brought something to the rodeo that the cowboys did not. They brightened up the dusty scene with a touch of glamor.

Even if they were going out to wrestle steers, the cowgirls always gave careful thought to their appearance. "We all had lots of clothes," one woman said. "We always wore our best clothes, no matter what we were doing." In those days, many of the cowgirls designed and made their own fancy western costumes. Some of them traveled from rodeo to rodeo with their sewing machines. When they were not riding broncs, they spent their time sewing and embroidering. They wanted people to see that they were typical young women who liked attractive clothes and who also happened to be exceptionally good at rodeo.

The crowds were thrilled by the sight of a girl on the back of a bucking horse. But the mood changed very quickly if she was injured. The rodeo was dangerous. Every day brought its share of sprained wrists, broken bones, and concussions. Every now and then a cowboy or cowgirl was killed.

Annie Oakley was a born entertainer. She never just walked into the arena. Instead, as one fan reported, "she tripped in, bowing, waving, and wafting kisses. Her first few shots brought forth a few screams of fright from the women, but they were soon lost in round after round of applause."

Above: DENVER PUBLIC LIBRARY, WESTERN HISTORY DEPARTMENT; Facing page: BUFFALO BILL HISTORICAL CENTER, CODY, WYOMING, GIFT OF THE COE FOUNDATION

Little Sure Shot

In the 1920s, many people thought that strong, active women were unfeminine. By tying their hair up in ribbons and wearing fancy clothes, the cowgirls tried to show that athletic women could also be beautiful. In doing this, they were following the lead of the very first cowgirl performer–Annie Oakley. Unlike most of the rodeo cowgirls, Annie Oakley did not grow up on a ranch. Instead, she was born in 1860 to a poor family in Ohio. "From the time I was nine," she once told a friend, "I never had a nickel I did not earn myself." As a girl, she earned money by shooting grouse and rabbits to sell to restaurants. That is how she developed her skill with a shotgun–the skill that would eventually lead her to fame and fortune in show business.

In 1885, Annie was hired to perform in a Wild West Show, a kind of western-themed circus that was very popular in the late 1800s. She dazzled audiences by shooting the ash off a lit cigarette or by aiming at targets from the back of a galloping horse. Although some people thought it was unnatural for a female to exhibit such skills, Annie did her best to demonstrate that she was a "true woman." She rode sidesaddle, did embroidery, and wore her hair in soft curls; she always dressed like a lady. This combination of skill and femininity made Annie Oakley a star—the most famous cowgirl performer of all time.

BONNIE McCARROL THROWN FROM

Everyone was distressed when a cowboy died, but they could generally accept the loss. They knew that he had died doing something he loved. But people became much more disturbed when a cowgirl lost her life. They thought of her as someone's daughter or wife. Young women should be taken care of, they said, and prevented from taking risks.

Over the years, a handful of cowgirl bronc riders were killed at the rodeo and, with each death, the organizers became more uncomfortable. By the late 1930s, they decided that women should not be allowed to compete in what was again seen as a man's sport, and in 1941 the last remaining ladies' bronc-riding competition was canceled. From then on, cowgirls were hired to appear in parades and put on riding shows to entertain the crowds at major rodeos. After little more than thirty years, the golden age of the rodeo cowgirl had come to a close.

A RODEO OF THEIR OWN

The cowgirls were not happy about this turn of events. They thought women should be allowed to make decisions for themselves. So, in 1947, a group of cowgirls in Amarillo, Texas, organized a rodeo of their own—the first All Girl Rodeo. The competitors roped steers and calves; they rode broncs and even bulls. They did all the things that people said girls should not do. "The stands were packed

Above: Vera McGinnis was completely battered and broken by the hooves of a bucking horse, but she never tired of rodeo. "I can honestly say the glamor never faded," she wrote. NATIONAL COWGIRL HALL OF FAME, FORT WORTH, TEXAS

Facing page: In 1915, bronc rider Bonnie McCarroll took a tumble off Silver but got up and walked away. Years later, she was not so lucky. Riding with her stirrups hobbled, she got caught in her gear and was killed. DENVER PUBLIC LIBRARY, WESTERN HISTORY DEPARTMENT

every night," one of the contestants said. "It was the best rodeo we ever had."

In addition to the thrills and spills of the traditional ranch sports, the All Girl Rodeo introduced an exciting new event. The idea of "riding barrels" had first come from the decorative shows that cowgirls were hired to put on at major rodeos. The riders were sometimes asked to ride their horses around barrels, in loops and figure eights, and even to turn their show into a race. For racing, the barrels were arranged in a large triangle so the women could ride around them in a clover-leaf pattern. One by one the competitors would thunder in, speed around the first pair of barrels in a tight figure-eight, gallop the length of the arena, make a quick loop around the final barrel, race back down the middle and out the entrance. Marks were supposed to be awarded for speed and subtracted for toppling the barrels, but the organizers did not make a serious attempt to keep score. The timing of the racers was sloppy, and the barrels were moved between runs. The "winner" was often the girl whom the judges found prettiest.

The cowgirls were determined to turn barrel racing into a real sport, with rules, regulations, and stopwatches. First prize would go to

Above: Rounding a barrel at a pounding gallop, Faye Blackstone demonstrates the style that made her a champion barrel racer in the 1950s. National Cowgirl Hall of Fame, Fort Worth, Texas

Facing page: Vera McGinnis claimed to have been the first woman to wear pants in the rodeo arena. She designed this Spanish-style outfit for a rodeo in London, England, in 1924. National Cowgirl Hall of Fame, Fort Worth, Texas

The All Girl Rodeo

This story about the first All Girl Rodeo comes from Texas cowgirl Fern Sawyer.

I wasn't entered in the bull riding but one night they didn't have anybody to ride a bull 'cause everybody was hurt. I told them I would do it because the crowd deserved to see a bull ride. My Daddy just had a fit. The last thing I saw before my ride was Daddy peeking through the fence. He said, "Well, if you get on him, you sure better ride him." I did ride him, but I broke my hand in nine places. I didn't get bucked off. I broke it gripping so hard.

the fastest rider who could gallop around all three barrels without upsetting them.

There are still a few women who ride broncs and bulls, but most rodeo cowgirls these days concentrate on barrel racing. If you go to the big Finals Rodeo in Canada or the United States, you will see them at their best, as the top competitors of the year race for the championship. The winner takes her stand among the year's rodeo champs—a proud representative of the cowgirl tradition.

THE SPIRIT LIVES ON

The world has changed, and changed again, since the cowgirl's story began, but her dauntless spirit is still with us. You find it at the rodeo and out on the range, but you are just as likely to find it in towns and cities. If you love wide open spaces—and the friendship of a good horse—then the spirit of the cowgirl is alive in your own heart. It lives in every girl who knows what she can do and who has the courage to make her dreams come true. The secret of happiness, Fannie Sperry once said, "is to do what you want to do, so long as you don't hurt anyone doing it." That is true cowgirl wisdom.

The Freedom of the Saddle

When Fannie Sperry was eighty-eight years old, she looked back on her long and satisfying life in the saddle.

Now that I am what young people consider an old woman, and I look back at my life, I can truthfully say that if I had it all to do over again, I would live it exactly the same. From such a statement you gather that I have liked it. I have *loved* it. And if, with my present arthritis, I must pay the price of every bronc ride that I have made, then I pay for it gladly. Pain is not too great a price to pay for the freedom of the saddle and a horse between the legs.

GLOSSARY

Arabian: A breed of sleek, fast horse.

Barbed wire: Wire armed with sharp points, used for making fences.

Barrel race: A race in which riders and their horses run a tight clover-leaf pattern around three barrels that are arranged in a triangle.

Brand: A mark of ownership that is burned into the hide of a horse or cow with a tool called a branding iron.

Breaking horses: Taming horses so they can be ridden.

Breeches: Britches, pants.

Bridle: A horse's headgear, used to control the animal.

Bronc: Short for bronco, a wild horse.

Buckskin: Tanned deerskin, used to make clothes.

Bulls: Adult male cattle that have not been castrated.

Calf: A young cow or bull.

Castrate: Cut out the testicles to turn a bull into a steer.

Cayuse: A wild horse.

Chute: A narrow passageway, like a hallway, with fences on either side.

Cinch: A band that goes under the belly of a horse to hold the saddle in place.

Colt: A young male horse.

Corral: A small fenced area where cows or horses are held.

Cowhand: A person who knows how to work with cattle; a cowgirl or cowboy.

Cow ponies: Small, fast horses that are used for working with cattle.

Cows: Cattle in general, or female cattle in particular.

Farm: Land that is plowed and used for raising crops.

Filly: A young female horse.

First Nations: People who lived in North America before the Europeans arrived.

Foal: A baby horse.

Foreman: The head of a work crew.

Gelding: A male horse that has been castrated.

Hand: See Cowhand.

Lariat: A rope with a noose, used for catching horses and cattle.

Livestock: Horses, cattle, or sheep.

Mare: A female horse.

Maverick: A calf that has not been branded.

Morgan: A slender, strong breed of horse.

Nag: A worn-out old horse.

Outlaw: A horse that cannot be tamed.

Petticoat: A skirt worn under dresses.

Plug: A worn-out old horse.

Prairie wool: Short, curly prairie grass.

Ranch: Land that is not plowed and that is used for raising livestock.

Range: Open, unfenced prairie.

Relay race: A race in which riders change horses several times.

Reservation, reserve: Land set aside for First Nations people.

Roan: A horse with a base coat of black, brown, or reddish hair, heavily intermixed with white.

Rodeo: A tournament of ranch sports.

Round-up: An organized attempt to find all the cattle that are pastured in a certain area and bring them together for branding or sorting.

Saddlehorn: A knob, or handle, at the front of a western saddle, used for mounting and dismounting and for carrying lariats and other gear.

Sampler: A piece of embroidery, often framed and displayed on the wall.

Sidesaddle: A woman's saddle that has been designed so the rider's legs are on the same side of the horse.

Six-gun: A type of gun, commonly used in the early West, that can be fired six times without reloading.

Sorrel: A reddish-brown horse.

Split-skirt: Pants with very wide legs.

Spread: A ranch.

Spurs: Sharp points buckled to the heels of cowboy boots, used by a rider to make a horse speed up or pay attention.

Steer: A bull that has been castrated.

Stetson: A broad-brimmed, high-crowned felt hat, often worn by cowhands.

Stirrups: The footrests attached to a saddle.

Stock: Short for livestock.

Stock horses: Horses that are used for working with cattle.

Thoroughbred: A breed of light, fast horse, often used for racing.

Western saddle: A saddle with a broad seat and a saddlehorn, designed for riding astride and working with cattle.

FOR MORE INFORMATION

Books

Annie Oakley and Buffalo Bill's Wild West by Isabelle S. Sayers (Dover, 1981) traces the remarkable career of Annie Oakley. Clear, informative text and lots of pictures.

Calamity Jane by Calamity Jane (Applewood, 1997) reproduces Calamity's account of her own life and adventures, as it was first published in 1896.

Cowgirl Legends: From the Cowgirl Hall of Fame by Kathy Lynn Wills and Virginia Artho (Gibbs-Smith, 1997) provides photos and short biographies of more than four dozen rodeo stars.

Cowgirls: 100 Years of Writing the Range by Thelma Poirier (Red Deer College Press, 1997) brings together poems and stories by more than fifty ranch women, including Evelyn Cameron, Monica Hopkins, and Belle Starr.

Cowgirls: Women of the American West by Teresa Jordan (University of Nebraska Press, 1992) is a collection of interviews with women who grew up on ranches in the United States. Great anecdotes about working with horses.

Girl on a Pony by LaVerne Hanners (University of Oklahoma Press, 1994) is a warm, funny book about growing up on a frontier ranch.

Letters from a Lady Rancher by Monica Hopkins (Goodread Biographies, 1983) provides a chatty and entertaining account of life on a ranch in Alberta in the early 1900s.

No Life for a Lady by Agnes Morley Cleaveland (University of Nebraska Press, 1977) is the autobiography of a woman who grew up on a ranch in New Mexico in the 1880s. Exciting and sometimes very funny.

Photographing Montana 1894-1928: The Life and Work of Evelyn Cameron by Donna M. Lucey (Alfred A. Knopf, 1991) showcases the photography and experiences of Montana rancher Evelyn Cameron.

Rodeo Road: My Life as a Pioneer Cowgirl by Vera McGinnis (Hastings, 1974) is the fast-paced and sometimes terrifying story of a much-honored—and much-injured—rodeo cowgirl.

Those Magnificent Cowgirls: A History of the Rodeo Cowgirl by Milt Riske (Wyoming Publishing, 1983) is just what the title suggests. Packed with interesting stories and historical photos.

Videos

The *Annie Oakley* television series first appeared in the 1950s as an action-adventure story with a sharp-shooting, hard-riding heroine. Despite the passage of time, it's still fun. Available from Shokus Video (www.shokus.com/annie.html).

"I'll Ride That Horse!" Montana Women Bronc Riders is a 27-minute program that features interviews with rodeo cowgirls. Includes historical rodeo photos and film of actual competitions. Available—for a price—from Women Make Movies: phone 1-212-925-0606 or Internet: www.wmm.com.

Websites

The HayNet (www.haynet.net) provides links to more than 11,000 websites about horses. Includes a special section for kids.

The National Cowgirl Museum and Hall of Fame in Fort Worth, Texas, can be contacted through their website (www.cowgirl.com).

The Personal HorsePages Webring (www.webring.org/cgi-bin/navcgi?ring=horsepages;list) offers a selection of pages about individuals and their horses.

The Professional Women's Rodeo Association is an organizaton of women who compete in bronc riding, bull riding, and roping (www.wpra.com/pwra1.html).

The Women's Professional Rodeo Association oversees barrel racing in the United States. The organization's website (www.wpra.com) provides information about the top American cowgirls of the year, as well as listings of upcoming competitions.

The Canadian Girls Rodeo Association can be reached by mail at Box 6152, Postal Station D, Calgary, Alberta T2P 2C8.

SOURCES

pp. 7–8, Fannie Sperry Steele, as told to Helen Clark, "A Horse Beneath Me Sometimes," *True West* (Jan-Feb 1976), pp. 8, 9, 11; p. 14, Georgie Sicking, "Just Thinking," unpublished ms, 1985, p. 1; p. 15, Agnes Morley Cleaveland, *No Life for a Lady*, pp. 66, 68; p. 15 (freedom), LaVerne Hanners, *Girl on a Pony*, pp. 92–93; p. 16, Thelma Poirier, unpublished ms, n.p.; p. 17 (interesting life), Elsie and Amy Cooksley, as quoted by Teresa Jordan, *Cowgirls: Women of the American West*, p. 12; p. 18, "Life and Adventures of Calamity Jane by Herself," in Roberta Beed Sollid, *Calamity Jane: A Study in Historical Criticism*. Western Press, 1958, pp. 125, 126, 129, 130; p. 19 (divided garments), Evelyn Cameron, as quoted by Donna M. Lucey, *Photographing Montana*, p. 204; p. 19 ("little ladies"), Ann Bassett Willis, "'Queen Ann' of Brown's Park," *Colorado Magazine* (Apr 1953), pp. 94–95; pp. 23, 24, E. Cameron, *Photographing Montana*, pp. xii, 90; p. 25 (cattleman on L. Williams), Ann Fears Crawford and Crystal Sasse Ragsdale, *Women in Texas: Their Lives, Their Experiences, Their Accomplishments*. State House, 1992, p. 120; p. 26 (roughing it), Elinore Pruitt Stewart, as quoted by Jordan, *Cowgirls*, p. 63; p. 26 (men spouting advice), unidentified woman homesteader, as quoted by Ruth Ann Alexander, "South Dakota Women Writers and the Blooming of the Pioneer Heroine, 1922–39," *South Dakota History* 14 (1984), p. 305; p. 27, *No Life for a Lady*, p. 103; pp. 28–29, Samuel Dunn Houston, "When a Girl Masqueraded as a Cowboy and Spent Four Months on the Trail," *The Trail Drivers of Texas*, ed. J. Marvin Hunter, New York: Argosy-Antiquarian, 1963, pp. 71–77; p. 30 (riding bareback), Dora Rhoads Waldrop, *Cowgirl Legends from the Cowgirl Hall of Fame*, p. 98; p. 30 (gathering horses), *No Life for a Lady*, pp. 65, 66; p. 33, Monica Hopkins, *Letters from a Lady Rancher*, pp. 89–90; pp. 34–35, E. Cameron, *Photographing Montana*, p. 88; p. 36, Elsie and Amy Cooksley, as quoted by Jordan, *Cowgirls*, p. 11; p. 36, Fannie Sperry Steele, as quoted by Vi and Marg Branders in Chris McGonigle, "The Six Sisters of the Circle Star Rodeo," *Mountain Rider* (Aug-Sept 1994), p. 3; p. 40 (B. Kapernick), as quoted by Mary Lou LeCompte, *Cowgirls of the Rodeo: Pioneer Professional Athletes*, University of Illinois Press, 1993, pp. 40–41; p. 40 (joy of living), May Lillie, as quoted by Glenn Shirley, *Pawnee Bill: A Biography of Major Gordon W. Lillie*, Western Publications, 1994, p. 187; p. 41, letter to Fannie Sperry, as quoted by Dee Marvine, "Fannie Sperry Wowed 'Em at First Calgary Stampede," *American West* (Aug 1987), p. 30; p. 48, "A Horse Beneath Me Sometimes," p. 27; p. 50 (clothes), Tad Lucas, as quoted by Jordan, *Cowgirls*, p. 76; pp. 50, 51 (A. Oakley), as quoted by Sayers, *Annie Oakley and Buffalo Bill's Wild West*, pp. 19, 4; p. 53 (V. McGinnis), as quoted by Le Compte, *Cowgirls of the Rodeo*, p. 31; pp. 53–54 (best rodeo), 55, Fern Sawyer, as quoted by Jordan, *Cowgirls*, pp. 230, 23; p. 56, F. Sperry, as quoted by Helen Clark, "Grand Old Lady of Rodeo: Fanny Sperry Steele," *Western Horseman* (Sept 1959), p. 59; p. 57, F. Sperry, "A Horse Beneath Me Sometimes," p. 12.

INDEX